This book is heavy on subject matter. It's not a read intended for individuals of weak stomach or who are unable to cope with the destruction of identity. Truth is not beautiful, and this book's intention is for awakening individuals from their delusions.

All the content in this book was written in 2018-2019; this was a period of self-realization through introspection and meditation. By deconstructing my own beliefs and social conditioning, I was able to breakthrough and witness life without judgment or preconceived notions; what I found was that life is beyond any human's understanding and that the vast majority of information we absorb since birth is based upon falsehoods.

Thank you for choosing to use your limited time in this world to read this book.

Dedication

Afton, you were one of the first individuals who made me feel validated and thanks to your kind words all of these ideas have flourished into trees.

Acknowledgment

Ed, thank you for being my friend and for helping me best communicate my thoughts into written words.

Lucidity

Perfection is the only word that wishes to appear before me as I gaze beyond my own sense of self. My greatest desire as a lost soul within this world was to find wisdom. It was a journey of seeking, to find salvation within the chaos of mortality. Truth is not beautiful. To become spiritually awakened you must be willing to face the depths of darkness. Beyond pain, confusion and isolation exists an awareness that cannot be spoken of, only experienced. To know true wisdom is to know that there is no longer a search for answers or to desire greater knowledge. What will be will always be and our discontentment with our lives comes from our necessity to become something we are not rather than being what we are.

If Enlightenment exists, it is a state of acknowledgment and acceptance of the circumstances you experience; the lawlessness of life no longer wavers your spirit.

The folly of mankind is believing that we are all created equally; we are nothing more than spiritual beings trapped within idealistic notions of right and wrong. A lion does not chew grass and a lamb does not hunt lions. We and the state of the world are designed as intended, whether the world is ideal or not is a matter of judgment and not divinity. The bleakest moments of human consciousness reveal that there is no inherent meaning to life. There is no god, there is no truth and all that remains is an unsettling silence. Either we will crumble beneath the destruction of our expectations or ascend beyond the fallacies of our ignorance.

Humanity is a void filled of pride and vanity. We toil and compete against one another for a place beneath the sun. And yet we remain blind to the magnitude of life and the insignificance of our worries. Mankind is foolish. We fight meaningless battles against one another only to extend our survival for a short period of time and still there is no escape from death. Philosophy is beyond thought, it is a way of action and motion within a world full of challenges. To be lucid within a world full of dreamers, is to know how interconnected life is. Every choice we make can change the lives of others for the better or worst.

There are no words that can awaken a mind, only an idea that reaches the human heart will change the way we choose to exist. It is my choice to walk into the void of existence, to confront the end and the beginning of life, and to understand the emptiness we all experience. Know that you are not alone, for as long as my words remain a part of this world, I will never leave you.

Life is but a leaf on an Autumn day

Within me, butterflies squirm against my stomach; they nuzzle their blue wings against my interior lining; I am nothing but a stone caterpillar trapped within its own nest. It is not me that is caught within emotional turmoil; the platter of small angels caged inside me are in pain. If they could vocalize words, they would only scream. I'm stitched together by tiny incandescent shapes; each word is like a chain and together they form the fibers of my self-woven prison.

Silly me, it's a theater within my imagination that trusts in the idea of romance. To be social, sharing thoughts through the rhythmic rattling of air that expels from my lungs; ending the hours of soliloquies and curiosity regarding the question, 'if it is better to be or not to be'; I would cease to be Hamlet. The hours of madness may disappear as the curtain closes on the performance on stage. Finished, yet the show would continue, one ticket for admittance and a lifetime of irreversible memories. The removal of my armor while standing in a field of armed archers; fearing the inevitable piercing of an arrow through my throat.

I am nothing but a fool caught within the terrors of rational outcomes. Before me is a painting of blood stained corpses, both men and women; my eyes meet their lips, smiles and frowns illustrated on every unanimated face. What did those lifeless individuals value during their short stay on Earth? Was the chance to lock eyes and meet a shared fate with another person meaningful enough for those men and women? Humanity exudes from this depiction of life captured by brush strokes and paint. There is a choice; either to leap into the pile of listless souls or find my own path. A world where I can overcome the thoughts placed into my head by human existence.

A chance to find meaning within the boundaries of meaninglessness; not to be consumed by the expectations of my society. To end the perpetual narrative of home and family; to rise above what children are told to believe is necessary and righteous. To not enslave another human by your ideals and to call them your legal possession. Or else, we live a simple life and fall into a deep unconscious sleep. Telling ourselves that we are correct for living an ideal, to own a house and a lover, and possessing temporary comforts that will return to dust.

Realms that exist outside the boundary of visible light; is life easier if we close our own eyes? Listen to the rustle of branches when a small gust of wind blows. Only moments pass by, and yet, what is time when you are shaken about by an outside force? Reflecting upon what is real, only to know that my voice speaks to those who cannot hear. My pupils absorb the refracted beams of reality; no matter the profundity of my screams, no one knows what I'm saying. I surmise that there cannot be a sense of lost within direction, if my path has not been chosen. If what I say can only be written, then this idea may remain if my heart becomes frozen. It is not that there is no heat within my furnace, but, wood should not be incinerated without purpose, and a blanket is sometimes more preferable than a warm room.

On a mountain, caught between a cliff and a lion, there is no denying the surge of life that follows. Would you fall off the edge, or wait for the inevitable conclusion? All paths always lead to the same denouement. A final destination exists and no earthly being can escape what was intended from conception. To know what awaits isn't torturous. Clarity comes from knowing. A mind that can acknowledge possibilities is only in conflict with itself; the fears it believes possible will only flourish under its foresight. It is not the world that creates our nightmares, but it is ourselves who maneuver this show.

Pleasure, wealth and luxuries are insignificant through the eyes of a holy person. Most humans aren't born with a desire to conceptualize existence beyond the material plane. Thoughts within me wander towards infinity; imagining countless stars that have disappeared; fantasizing over heavenly bodies that have yet to coalesce; all that is here today will vanish and be forgotten tomorrow. Life is transient; and most humans dismiss this axiom, thus humans spend the vast hours of their waking moments contemplating. They are never truly alive in the present moment, but lost in the grasp of the future and past. Our world is brimming with brilliant men and women. Sentient beings whose lives are forsaken in the quest for control and certainty.

A human being who desires to control the world around them, suffers from their own insecurity. To have absolute power does not guarantee peace; it is a pathway full of challenges.

Sovereignty rewards any one person with earthly treasures of flesh and jewels. If we peer into the furthest reaches of our civilized world, you will easily find those who crave the prize of authority; to dictate our terrestrial game and to find false fulfillment through external prestige. It is rare to encounter a being who does not strive for physical rewards or merits. I am nothing, neither a righteous saint nor perverse creature; a corporeal being who sees no noble or condemnable way to act as a human. Thus it is lawful for all to desire strength and glory, or humility and meekness.

There are no instructions or words of wisdom that are prescribed as canon for all. We know of nothing, yet we all continue to breathe without effort. It's utterly foolish to not become consumed by your possessions; and perfectly wise to abandon all conceptions of ownership. Humanity does not thrive without staining its hands red. It is our privilege to reap what has been sowed. This image of life is tragic, consumption of all until self-annihilation is achieved. No one is at fault. Our framework of civilized life is destructive, and after all is said, go and liberate yourself through your desires; conquer, pillage, create, and fulfill your potential as a being who draws in breath.

The purpose of life is not for us to erect everlasting monuments or to uncover esoteric knowledge. Nothing is intended to remain, all that we covet is of earthly concerns. To experience life is to breathe, there is no mystery nor direction. There are no secrets, only illusions that we perpetuate. I say to thee, let all who can hear, cast aside their sense of self and become empty.

All that we do is utterly pointless; enter the void and let it consume you. My message is cruel and silly to a degree; yet, there is so much beauty in writing about meaninglessness. In the chasm of no meaning, there is only meaning to be found; meaning cannot arise until you ascribe it for yourself. If you never allow for the destruction of your ego, how will you ever become reborn? Too many humans are trapped within an idealistic fallacy about life. They believe in concepts such as honor, pride, truth, justice and so forth; virtues are nothing but man-made ideals; they are beautiful, but they cannot endure within the realm of meaninglessness.

It is not that we should be saddened by how insignificant our lives are; only that we must rejoice and understand how frivolous all our fears and delusions are. Why do we ever worry, when, the larger scope of reality is all but a dismal abyss? Why do humans fear for their pointless lives, when, all that lies on the other side is the same inevitable conclusion, we were born to die. Gloom is within me, but it is not a dark feeling. Gloom is the bucket filled with paint which splashes pink blossoms onto a white canvas. Humans must embrace their fragile lives, there is no answer other than to live your only life.

We are free to contemplate the corruption and injustice that is aligned with existence; arguing and senselessly fighting a war against all supposed oppressors; hoping to change the world into a paradise. What is paradise if not a conception of a human ideological framework? Humans have a choice. Some humans can enjoy the advantages of privilege while another set of humans experience the extreme opposite. Or all humans can abide within a frame of existence in which all men and women become commodities; we can cease to be individuals and become a herd of sheep living for our day to day sustenance. There aren't any reasons to continue with our day to day worries; you, the stars, our yellow sun, and myself will one day vanish into nothingness. For life to perish, that is not one of my concerns; for life to continue or not, neither is it my concern.

My body is a living corpse slowly perpetuating itself between life and death; nearing one end of the spectrum closer and closer. Existing within the bosom of eternity is enrapturing. The world swirls without making my insides feel motion sickness; hours and minutes leap from one position into another, yet there is no sound of a ticking clock. All we know for certain is that one day the grand curtain will close upon us. We will exit the world's stage and cease to be. There is so much to do during a lifetime, but what is worth doing?

A sad girl sitting by a calm river

It troubles me that our civilization is too focused on the idea of finding happiness. It is not that I am not happy, but more as if I do not understand happiness; my mind and soul surge through waters of emotional torrents; mellow clouds position themselves above me as I place my essence into this text. Life has become a process in which humans strive towards the outlandish goal of acquiring happiness. It's odd that happiness alludes me, but to a child, happiness is an essential part of life.

What do I carry within me that prevents myself from feeling total bliss? Is there pain within me that hides itself like a shadow within the dark? Do I carry my pain as a shield and deny the world around me? There have been days in which I succumbed to the thought process of dying by my own hands; there was an allure of wonder within me that pondered upon the feel of a sharp blade against my flesh; don't misinterpret me, I was curious to know the sensations that are provided from the experience. My smooth flesh is of a pleasant texture and yet I wondered what the irrevocable cause of a self-inflecting wound would feel like. These thoughts are pondered not because I'm a danger to myself; only that I dared to ask and question what others may not allow themselves to.

I'm unconcerned with regards to whether I am right or wrong for thinking the way I do. Within our minds, we are prisoners to our own imagination. No person is a prisoner of society until they act upon the thoughts which constitute their mind. For true growth, shouldn't an individual delve deep into the realm of thought which is counter aligned with their normal framework? What is meaning, to someone who cannot see life for more than a mirage with circumstances derived by a society? Our time is spent striving for achievements that serve no purpose; suddenly we vanish and all that we gained slips from our ephemeral hands.

I despise the self-indulgence of sorrow and misery. The sensation of drowning within air feels incomparable; you will continuously inhale air no matter what vicious pain is encountered; it's a standstill between you and the figments of your thoughts; how conscious can you become to slip past the dreaded wall of temporal existence? Come to me dear reader, can you smell the scent of stale emotions that linger from within? There is no sense in you hiding what's inside of yourself; let it out and scream what you feel. Go ahead, shout and let the world hear you, everyone around you will perish either way. Be heard and not denied of your right to vocalize. Nothing matters, regardless of what I say or do, watch as time unfolds before both of us; please gain perspective regarding how insignificant life can be at any given moment; how could you know what carries significance if you can't observe how unimportant everything can be?

It is not the role of any one individual to manifest hope into the soul of another. Truth must be exposed. No longer should any man, woman or being, live within the illusions of social conditioning; we must all be liberated of our self-imposed unconscious behaviors and manifest change within ourselves. Any society that remains unconscious of self, hinders their collective-preservation; our responsibility is not to simply be alive, but to exist consciously within the void of an infinite abyss.

Truth is spoken with the intention of awakening a slumbering segment of the human intellect. Truth is not beautiful. What is truthful will arise an internal fear; either the individual will address their fear and overcome it, or they will be subjugated to their willingness of remaining ignorant. No one should remain a slave to fear, we have to rise up and focus on what is at hand. Our world will remain as a perpetual state of meaninglessness if we do not take action. To explore the concept of meaninglessness is to provide evidence that not taking action or not exerting effort is more meaningless than meaninglessness. All of life is temporary and you must discover meaning for yourself. Abandon all that you

know and determine your own reason for being alive.

Simplicity is a remedy to cure the disease of knowledge

Let my soft rigid words enter your entangled mind. What I speak of holds no significance if you are not able to understand. It is not you or I who decide, but those who have been endowed with the privilege to hear, will. You are living within an ever changing story; an intricate web fabricated by multiple narratives. What you see in front of you and all around you, are lies. Truth is a lie, reality is an illusion. No matter how deep we go into ourselves or the world around us; every aspect of our life is a falsity.

If this exact moment is an illusion, you must come to realize that every moment before it was also false. When I speak of an illusion or life not being real I am speaking about our limited capacity to understand, whatever happens is only a narrow perception of what could truly be. There is a false narrative occurring within the consciousness of every living being, or humans to say the least. I stare at the creatures around us and wonder what type of hypnosis animals exist within. It is not that humans are conscious beings, only, that they have altered their state of hypnosis from that of a brutal beast to that of a quivering branch. All humans are sleeping within their own slice of heaven or hell, to think, is only to become a spectator within a performance.

To those who believe that consciousness is a state of self-actualization one must ask themselves; what is consciousness or awareness? What is truth and what is the ultimate state of reality? I ask these questions, not as if I have an answer or a conclusion, even though I may appear to be conscious from within. It is of utmost importance for you, the reader, to understand that I am not omnipotent and therefore I am only a single droplet within an ocean of wisdom. You have to radically train your mind to understand that wisdom, enlightenment, knowledge and all other idealized states are temporary. To have the capacity to overcome your past self is an extraordinary quality. The deeper you go towards finding truth, you come to a conclusion that truth is a praised ideal that does not exist; or it may, who am I to declare absolute authority over what anyone may believe.

What I see within our earthly realm is that our thoughts create the reality we exist within. The stories we internalize make us who we are. It is as if we exist within a realm of infinite possibilities. Slowly the world and ourselves change, but it is only after waiting that we can actualize what we believe is possible. Here in my mind, I see our existence and know that all is possible, all is meaningless, yet, nothing is impossible.

Meaninglessness, oh dear, how I use the word so loosely. I hope fragility isn't written on your forehead. Where we are going is not a safe place for the ego. If I could rip apart your sense of self, I would. Who you think you are is nothing more than a lie. What you believe is important may as well be insignificant, but, we live in a manner in which we seek purpose and self fulfillment. People throw away the hours of their days watching movies or reading books, never truly knowing why they give themselves away to mental stimulation.

If I dared to deeply care, I would ask myself why I dare to dream or dare to do anything. I would stand outside in the cold fully aware that life isn't about contemplation; life isn't a riddle we should convulse over. The way we feel and what we think are utterly pointless, therefore, we must continue and abandon who we are. Solace does not exist within thoughts, only in the warmth of sunlight and the arms of a loved one. Do not overlook what is simple.

A gap between nothingness and infinity

Enter the void and leave all earthly attachments behind. I hear these words resonating within the depths of my being. I forsake my body and my mind to enter the emptiness of existence. That which is me was once nothing, neither a seed nor a thought, my birth is nothing more than a mere probability and occurrence of events outside of my control.

My essence submits to that which is eternal. No thoughts, religions, drugs or addictions will keep me from embracing the ungraspable. To seek emptiness is to allow the destruction of your identity and sense of self; to die over and over again until there is no point of reference. These thoughts of mine, for whom are they written? It is not my eyes that deceive me, only my mind. Light enters within my eyes, it is like a scene of black and white. What is true and what is false, are choices for you to decide.

No matter what I can conceptualize, the choice to understand is always an option. Humans can either see and react, or observe and let go. For what reasons do we intend to capture thoughts and latch onto them? Waves upon air crash within my mind. What is here and now feels magical and refreshing; detachment. I breathe in infinity and exhale the depths of life; my lungs fill up, this is a moment of reality collapsing upon itself; my ego detaches and I'm caught between infinity and emptiness. My one life, feels fulfilled within the expansiveness of existence. The experience of being beyond flesh and blood reverberates within my bones. To know what I feel is to drop a stone in a bottomless well.

The end of identity

There is no "I".

All humans are part of a systematic program which dictates what we know and think. We have been provided with the tools of language and words to identify the world around us. Through this commonality our minds are united; but we are limited by the syntax we know in order to define or perceive our reality. The rules that dictate how we think must have an origin point, but we have muffled this truth by disguising ourselves within a social system that manipulates our thoughts and behaviors.

The capacity to think is the ability to control words and place them in different sequences. A person who does not think or does not think deeply, does not bother with rearranging words to create new sentences or questions which lead to new ideas and insights. Words are symbols and they dictate how we experience our lives, how we identify ourselves and the world around us. The capacity to use words to understand consciousness and society is profound. Within every person there is a mind, and that mind only functions through the usage of words and other symbols. Without knowing words, a person cannot become a functioning member of society.

The premise of this insight is that words are the life force of a civilization. All humans are linked through their capacity to be programmed by language; except, life begins without language. No one was born with this ability, we were assimilated into this form of manipulation. There is a world beyond words and syntax, but, because our social system is designed to perpetuate its own existence, no infant can escape or survive without being hypnotized by external stimuli. When a child begins to know of words, they become indoctrinated into the unconsciousness of humanity. As a child develops and matures, they will either awaken to the realization of humans existing within a dreamlike hypnosis perpetuated by social structures or remain dreaming. If the social system allows for you to awaken, then you must understand that life is not comprehensible within the parameters of language or thoughts.

The world beyond syntax is ungraspable. You cannot define this form of truth, it may only be experienced and observed by an individual. Most people who have the privilege to think are not capable of turning off their thoughts. Through practice and patience, it is possible to turn off our internal dialogue and become immersed within the realm of silence. This is a range of perception where humans can bypass thoughts and observe the grandeur of existence. This realm is nothing more than an opportunity for an individual to see the interconnectedness of reality and the divisions caused by our social programming.

When the mind is silenced and words no longer reinforce the structure of reality, you become aware of humanity's foolishness. On a biological basis, all sentient beings are nothing more than clumps of earth. Our inherent difference from animals is that we exist with an overactive imagination which has transformed the planet. Without words, we cease to be individuals and can no longer construct an identity for ourselves or the world around us. All that remains is the water and soil all species depend upon. Thus, I must inform you, there is no sense of "I" or self beyond the existence of our social programming.

To know that we are all made from the same dirt is a humbling process. Without a society or civilization to dictate our thoughts, the world returns to its natural state. The reasoning behind kindness is nothing more than the acknowledgment of how misguided humanity remains. The anger and hatred experienced within this world are created by the perpetuation of the idea of separation. This grand illusion must meet its conclusion, humanity must understand that the divisions we believe in are nothing more than ideas created by our social programming. To know truth is to know that we are all born of the same dust and

we will all experience the cessation of life.

Running faster, do we race against the clock of humanity. We are constantly searching for an answer for all of our pain and suffering. I don't believe that humans want others to suffer, but living in ignorance is not a solution. Whether we are aware or not, life is full of suffering. To suffer does not indicate one narrow path of existence, this a doorway that opens an infinite realm of possibilities. One form of suffering is not the equivalent of all forms of suffering.

Shame, a word that runs and leaps over hurdles of dark truths. Light, a reflection from a mug of warm tea. We sit here together, acknowledging the endless chase created by society. All people of different colors and backgrounds line up together on a running track; each individual, trapped between white lines; a referee dressed in a black vestment fires a starting gun. Life, the beginning of a race, be with me, watch from above like sunlight and drink merrily.

A metaphor for a race would not make sense to a frog resting upon a lily pad. For a creature of the Earth, what is life other than a way of being? No toil nor rest for an animal, life is a state of existence. Mankind is another breed. Humans are chained and shackled by their thoughts, forever enslaved by a world perpetuated from within. To move and breathe is not enough, progress and advancement is valued more than life itself. While the slaves of civilization carry the weight of ideals, a world full of organic beings exist within the bliss of freedom. No thoughts of a future or a method for measurement, simply living for the sake of life.

Humans exist as if life were a technical error by some entity. The natural world is not enough for us and thus we must change it. We have eradicated a non-quantifiable amount of species due to their lack of convenience on behalf of our socially constructed expectations. Mankind has ceased to adapt to its world and instead has forced the world to adapt to it. Madness, civilization exists in a state of delirium. Systematically our species is mentally conditioned to pursue an existence that destabilizes the Earth. This is not a conspiracy but an observation of our collective education. Children are herded into factory like school systems which prepare them to take advantage of their society; brainwashed and forced to become better, our youth is lost within the paradigm of freedom and truth. Money is salvation and poverty is slavery, while this may be partially truthful, the inverse is just as honest.

There is no true error with life, only perfection and beauty exists. It is our civilized error that has caused our suffering. Almost all humans are habituated to compete against one another. It is only through our own efforts that we can supposedly find success within our world of culture and education. What is deemed correct is not always the path that leads to what we most desperately require. Surely, my thoughts are not capable of appeasing an empty stomach. My meditations do not serve the poverty stricken individuals who live only for the flesh, yet, I do not end my composition, for those who seek what is beyond the body have come here to be with me.

Do not spill your own ruby hued blood. I have become weary from watching my brethren run in circles attempting to cross a finish line that does not exist. Yes, you are flesh that carries sanguine fluid within your own arms and legs. It is unlikely that you will keep running without reaching a state of collapse. I weep and grieve that humanity has been fooled by structures that were intended to protect them. There is no security within the palisade that dictates our lives; you have been mislead and forced to exist within a state of constant torture. Your mind, the mind of mankind, is the vial that contains poison disguised as progress and reason.

Humanity sits upon a throne of hemic corpses. Our towers, institutions, and chapels are excuses for the condemnation of our shared world. A desolate tone of voice preaches for advancement. My fellow beings, there is no space for us within the kingdom of man. We are forced to walk this path and find our resting place amongst the carrion of those who came before us. Without proper illumination of our mortal existence, we will continue to lay bricks which build the confinement of future generations.

Our eyes grow accustomed to a sense of hunger. Feeding upon the visual stimulation of clothes, titles, money, can our cravings for imitation be satisfied? The root of our suffering comes from what we do not have and what our external environment determines we need. Would it be outlandish to say that humans are imprisoned by the necessities normalized by a society? To have what is not ours then becomes a mission; life is no longer an individual process, but a dictation to fulfill a social expectation. Focus sways from the lone mind of imaginary thoughts, influenced by a collective which has no sense of self. What is fulfilling and truthful becomes a standardization instead of a personal experience. And yet, humanity becomes harmonized through this mutual sense of self-torment. A human being can no longer ease their hunger unless they become what the world deems they should be, an illusion, only starvation will follow.

Through our journeys, filled with agony and pain, all of us search for freedom. An opportunity to escape the cage we have been placed into. Liberation is not a place that can be found or searched for, it is a state of being. Man cannot be satisfied by objects. Man must realize that there will never be peace without ceasing desire. Actualize yourself and observe how insignificant every aspect of life truly is, know meaninglessness and be content. Whether you prosper or diminish through the chains of civilization, freedom does not exist upon the material plane.

Gold, silver and diamonds are but pieces of earth, reflective compositions found buried within dirt. A mind that is full cannot understand the emptiness of jewelry. We are bits of dust who are taught to chase after imaginary concepts. The mundane tribulations that civilized beings face are what lead to symptoms which conspire against our own health. If we have not achieved a certain social expectation, we are deemed unworthy. If our life is not up to par with our peers, we see ourselves as failures. What we posses and who we are seen as, is as valuable as any precious stone or metal. This way of thinking, is nothing but a box for us to place ourselves into. Imaginary is the life we choose and wars will be fought to declare which box every being should live within.

What bothers me deeply, is the sense of imprisonment we carry for those around us. Each individual is taught to look at their neighbor and evaluate their position in life, whether it be consciously or subconsciously. We are molded to judge those around us for what they have and do not have. Worth does not become an issue of internal truth. Our personal significance is no longer based upon our existence, but whether our life contributes to the betterment of society. Thus, we strive to validate ourselves to a social system that dictates our beliefs and values.

A social system is a double-edged tool, as a collective we can achieve more; but collectively we learn to oppress each other. The fear of colliding with humans is at times too outlandish and egoistic; there is a pressure that is unspoken. One reason that humans conform to the expectations of a society is due to aversion of pain. It is not that we fear what others think, but we fear to lose our grip with how we identify our reality. Thus, we make an attempt to stabilize ourselves with what we believe is truthful.

Mankind is judged not by men and women, but by systems which dictate righteousness. Our world is small, and still, there are several different forms of beliefs. Humans will think and discuss, and attempt to find solutions to secular issues. What is fair, is a decision made by individuals with power. The disenfranchised have no say regarding truth and justice, they are victims to ideas actualized by their rulers. A society is established with the intention of improving the lives of its constituents. Institutions are erected to forward the progression of thought and welfare of all. This ideal for a virtuous collective existence is not practical, only theoretical. A royal palace is built with the intention of housing an exclusive group of individuals. Not everyone is allowed to enter. While the elite eat their fill, the rest of society holds up the pillars which stabilizes their kingdom. Thus, power is a privilege and is not intended for the masses.

Humanity is a satire directed by sunbeams

ACT 1
SCENE 1

Venus

Why is it that every time we meet up you've finished half a battle of wine?

Sophie

What? Are you involved with the CIA now? Building my profile or something?

Venus

No. I'm just concerned about your life choices.

Sophie

Relax, if I drink some wine, I'm just drinking some wine. Someone went to the trouble of making it, the least I can do is drink it.

Venus

That's not what I meant. You've been drinking ever since I met you.

Sophie

Yeah, I'm an adult. Adults can drink wine if they want to. I'm allowed to drink whenever I want. That's a perk of growing up.

Venus

So adulthood to you means drinking all the time?

Sophie

Not all the time, just when the clock flashes 5 o'clock. I leave one job and get to my next one. Drinking is a career on it's own.

Venus

How old were you when you had your first drink?

Sophie

You ask a lot of questions. Let's just get on with the show.

End of Act 1, Scene 1

Apollo

How can anyone bare to stand this ridiculous game?

Eos

What game? Is it the game where you hop on one leg while you rub your stomach and pat your head?

Apollo

No… that isn't the kind of game I'm talking about. Our life, that game.

Eos

Huh? Life isn't a game, there aren't any rules and a game isn't a game unless it has rules. You know what is a game? Tic-tac-toe! You have to connect 3 Xs or 3 Os in a line and then you win. You don't win at life, you just live it.

Apollo

Well… you have a good point.

Eos

Of course I do, I wouldn't speak if I didn't have reason not to.

Apollo

How do you cope with the stress of this unbearable burden?

Eos

How about you get on the floor and I'll show you.
(Eos helps Apollo lay down on the floor).

                    Eos
Okay, now start by taking in a deep breath and exhaling. Take
another breath and scream at the top of your lungs!
                (Apollo screams)

                    Eos
And that's all there is to it.

            (Eos helps Apollo get back up)

                    Apollo
So you just get on the floor and scream?

                    Eos
It helps doesn't it?

                    Apollo
You're right.

                    Eos
I got another idea, how about we play a game?

                    Apollo
What kind of game?

                    Eos
The rules are… we each take turns mimicking the other's
movements… and we can't talk… Here I'll show you, do what
ever I do.

        (Eos raises both of her arms into the air)

        (Apollo hesitantly follows along)

(Eos lowers her arms and points at Apollo to indicate that it is his turn)

(Apollo realizes it's his turn and starts flapping his arms like a bird)

(Eos flaps her arms)

(Eos places her hands on her hips and starts to sway from side to side)

(Apollo repeats the motion)

(Apollo grins and pulls out a rolling paper and lighter from his pant's pocket, he proceeds to light the rolling paper, smokes it and offers it to Eos)

(Eos looks at the rolling paper, looks at the audience then turns back and takes the paper and smokes it)

(Eos coughs and hands the paper back to Apollo)

Apollo
Bet you didn't see that one coming.

(Eos coughing)

(Apollo takes another hit)

Apollo
I call this game "let's not think about it".

Eos
You can't really call this a game, are there any rules?

                    Apollo
Of course there are rules, hit it and pass it, repeat until you have
to ash it.

                     Eos
Hmm… well if that's the game you want to play.

                (Apollo chuckles)

                    Apollo
This is my favorite game. I can spend hours playing this.

                     Eos
It doesn't seem like the healthiest of games.

                    Apollo
Who cares about health? We're all going to be worm food one
day.

                     Eos
Ew, I don't want to be worm food. I want my remains to be sent
into space, just so I can be amongst stars.

                    Apollo
It's inevitable, one day you're here next day you're something
else's meal. It can't be helped.

                     Eos
Is this why you're always feeling down?

                    Apollo
Not really. That's just a fact that I accept.

     (Apollo passes the rolling paper to Eos and Eos takes a hit)

Apollo

What would life be if it wasn't as absurd as living your whole life only to become food for the next guy…

(Eos coughs)

Eos

Don't you think there's more to life than just that?

Apollo

Not really.

Eos

That's unfortunate. I personally know that life is magic.

Apollo

If you say so…

Eos

No. Really. It is. You see, for me, there are no such things as coincidences. Only probability.

Apollo

What's the difference?

Eos

Saying that something is a coincidence is the same as giving up without trying. But, when you believe in probability, you give hope to what many may believe is impossible. When in fact, nothing is impossible.

Apollo

What about life? It's impossible to bare.

                         Eos
You live your life too seriously.

                        Apollo
How can I not? Everything is so messed up. Wars, hunger,
poverty, disease… just to name a few.

            (Eos passes the paper to Apollo)

                         Eos
So do you think being miserable will solve those issues? Because
it doesn't. Being miserable only causes more misery.

                  (Apollo laughs)

                        Apollo
You got a good point. I just can't get out of this state of mind.

                         Eos
It's not an instant process. It takes time and patience. Not being
miserable is like performing surgery on your own brain.

                        Apollo
Brain surgery?

                         Eos
Not brain surgery in particular, but reprogramming how you
think.
                        Apollo
What if I like the way I think?

                         Eos
How do you know you like it, if it's all you've ever known?

Apollo

Isn't that why I should like it?

(Apollo ashes the paper)

Eos

I don't think so. Just because you were taught to believe in something, doesn't mean it's wrong to change your beliefs. The leaves on an autumn tree change colors, that doesn't mean the leaves are wrong for not being green.

Apollo

So how do you go about "reprogramming your mind"?

Eos

It really depends. You can tell a child to be good, but that doesn't stop them from being mischievous. I can tell you all my secrets, but that doesn't mean you'll understand them.

Apollo

You're so vague, you start a conversation about changing how one thinks and you're not going to tell me?
(Eos giggles)

Eos

You're just like everyone else. Always wanting a set of instructions on how to do the most basic of functions. What does changing the way you think sound like to you?

Apollo

Thinking one way and then thinking another way.

Eos

That's a good start. Can you be a bit more explicit?

Apollo

It's like believing the sky is blue just because you can see it. Only to discover that the sky is actually black and humans perceive blue because of light particles being scattered by the Earth's atmosphere.

Eos

I think you get it.

Apollo

You sure? What exactly do I understand?

Eos

That nothing is ever as what it appears to be. Life is full of smoke and mirrors. If you hold onto any belief, you become as smokey and illusionary as that idea.

Apollo

So you think the right thing to do is to become ungrounded?

Eos

It's not the 'right' way to live, it's one way to live. Right or wrong means that there is a foundation for our beliefs. We're just humans, we create and perpetuate the reality that's right in front of us.

Apollo

You sound crazy. There is definitely a right way to live.

Eos

Me, crazy? You sound like a dictator. As soon as people incorporate the idea of righteousness, they allow oppression and narcissism to be born.

50

                              Apollo
Are you telling me, you want the world to be chaotic?

                               Eos
No, how did you arrive to that conclusion?

                              Apollo
You talk as if oppression isn't important.

                               Eos
What?! Are you the crazy one? Oppression is terrible! No one
deserves to be oppressed!

                              Apollo
I'm not crazy… but I don't think it's fair to be an idealistic
warrior. No society can function or thrive without someone being
'oppressed'. There will always be someone in charge and
someone cleaning up the messes.

                               Eos
Yeah! Only if you sit there and do nothing!

                              Apollo
Okay Madam. Describe to me your idealistic world.

                               Eos
Give me a minute.

(Eos paces in a circle. Apollo pulls out a stick of gum and starts
                           chewing it)

Eos

I got it! MY perfect world. Everyone is treated fairly and everyone cleans up after themselves. And there will be lots of colors, a bright and colorful world of justice!

Apollo

Don't you think that your sense of justice is an illusion?

Eos

I do, but that doesn't mean we shouldn't strive towards a better world. Did you have something better in mind?

Apollo

We should keep everything as it is. I don't really care about the chaos. When you really get down to it, our world is so diverse. If anything, we are at the peak of creative thinking. It's all down hill from here, imagine your perfect world becoming a reality. Thoughts would become regulated and creativity would become conformed, all for the sake of equality.

(Light dims, spotlight on Apollo. 9 soldiers march across the stage and exit)

Apollo

I can already hear the future. A world full of structure and limitations.

Eos

And what's wrong with structure?

Apollo

It makes the search for meaning, meaningless.

(Stage lights return to normal)

Eos

Is that why you're always gloomy? You're looking for meaning?

Apollo

I would hope so. Do you honestly think sending out job applications is more important than the grand scheme of life?

Eos

No… but...

(Apollo interrupts)

Apollo

You have to face it, the more structure that is created, the more miserable humans become. Do you think prehistoric humans had to deal with any of the bs we deal with today?

Eos

No… but do you think we would be better off, living in a world where people could raid your village in the middle of the night, slaughter your family and enslave the survivors? You think that's a better world to live in?

Apollo

Can we just agree that every way you look at life, it sucks.

Eos

No. I can't agree, well, at least not completely. Sure… I can agree that life isn't perfect. But that doesn't mean everything is terrible. Have you ever witnessed a sunset while sitting by a calm lake? There's a moment of perfection when you can see the sunlight reflecting an orange hue across the water. It makes Earth look like as if it were Mars. In a simple moment of beauty like that one, I can assure you that life isn't that bad.

Apollo
You're hilarious, how many people have the privilege of spending
their time by a lake?

Eos
Sure, you're right. I am privileged. But just because my moment
of happiness involves a lake, that doesn't mean someone else
doesn't have their own version of beauty. I don't know, maybe
someone feels really fortunate to have running water or
something! The point is, you can't live your life focusing on
everything that's terrible. You'll drive yourself insane.

Apollo
So you would rather be ignorant of the world around you?

Eos
Where do you come up with these conclusions? I'm just saying
that you have to live harmoniously. We're not here to solve every
issue, we are here to live.

Apollo
Yes, but as soon as you stop caring about every issue you allow
the world to slip into a mob of conformity. It's all or nothing.

Eos
Why do you care so much about what happens to the human race?

Apollo
I think about future generations and how they may never
experience the full potential of their humanity.

Eos
What full potential? There is no full human potential. Even today,
in your supposed paradise full of diversity. You have people who

are financially trapped into working jobs they hate and being married to people they kinda sorta like, because a divorce would be more expensive than staying together.

Apollo

No, not that kind of potential. I'm talking about having a world where kids can look up at the sky and dream of traveling to distant planets. A world where you can think big and not have to be afraid of being different. A place where you're allowed to be yourself.

Eos

You sound delusional. I understand that there are countries were you're killed for being different. But even in the countries were being different isn't a crime, humans have a natural tendency to conform. You don't need a dictator to tell people how to think. Individuals will police their own thoughts. Why pay someone to tell people what to think, when citizens will do it for free?

Apollo

You're never satisfied, are you?

Eos

I've just had a lot of time to think about how foolish humans can be.

Apollo

When was the last time you actually believed in something?

Eos

Probably when I thought I was in love. It felt real. But we were separated by our circumstances. Everything sort of fell apart. And I had a lot of time to think about how silly being human can be.

55

Apollo

How long ago was that?

Eos

Maybe 4 years. I stopped keeping track of it.

Apollo

Did you give up on them?

Eos

I was lost. To me, love is like holding onto a map and knowing exactly where you're heading. When I lost them, I lost the destination. So I tried to find something more suitable for me, something that wasn't definable by another person.

Apollo

What keeps you going each day then?

Eos

The pursuit of mystery.

Apollo

So you're living simply for the sake of mystery?

Eos

If there's a mystery that means there is always an adventure.

Apollo

Most people have a tendency to say that their purpose in life is to make lots of money or become really famous. You on the other hand, are quite a surprise.

Eos

What's the point of money or fame? To have them is pleasant, but I see those two more as side dishes rather than a main course. It's

56

not like we can take money with us when we die. And fame isn't that important, most of the people who know of you don't know you, but only an idea that you represent. You're only a fragment to others, never an entire identity.

Apollo

I wouldn't mind fame actually. Sure, no one really knows you. But, I wonder what it's like. You know, to be treated like you matter in a world full of nobodies. Everyone praises you and treats you like royalty.

Eos

Fame probably sounds nicer when you're the person doing the fawning and not when you're the person being fawned after.

Apollo

I doubt it, having everyone wanting your attention sounds great!

Eos

Popularity really means that much to you?

Apollo

Yeah. Some days are lonelier than others.

Eos

Just because people scream out your name and want to take photos with you, doesn't mean you won't be lonely.

Apollo

Maybe for you. But just to have that sense of being desired is all I need. Look at me, I'm out here being a nobody. Waiting and waiting. All we ever do is wait.

Eos

Then why not wait some more?

Apollo

You're not being helpful…

Eos

It's not like I can speed up time for you. Sometimes you have to accept that waiting is essential.

Apollo

I can't… I'm out of here…

(Apollo proceeds to leave. Eos remains alone)

Eos

Foolish boy (laughs)

Eos

We're all fictitious characters who pretend to have control of a mere shadow. Slowly applying adhesive tape onto a piece of paper; hoping that it remains bound to one point in existence. Yet, this folly is all we have and to say that there is no hope is devastating. If there was no more sun to lay the heavens in flames, what would we do? Alas, all of this is a mere dream in which we forget our lives. A mere fantasy which has subdued our inner being, thus leaving us in a perpetual state of agony.

(lights fade)

End of Act 1, Scene 2

ACT 2
SCENE 1

(At a restaurant)

Sophie

Now wasn't that a great way to start off our intricate
performance?

Venus

I have a deep inner sense that the majority of what is said during a
theatrical performance is lost to the audience.

(A waiter brings a bottle of wine and pours it into the glasses of
Venus and Sophie. Venus and Sophie thank the waiter)

Sophie

But who can blame the audience for not understanding? It's not
like everyone is consciously observing the performance as it was
intended by the playwright.

Venus

That's true, but you know what. I find absolute comfort in hearing
laughter from the audience. There is always a glimmer of hope,
that something the audience saw on stage struck deep within their
unconscious mind to make them laugh.

Sophie

You mean like when people see a cartoon about a cat hating
Mondays and the reader starts to laugh because they hate their
job?

Venus

Sort of like that. I believe that the unconscious mind laughs at what is relatable. A joke isn't funny if an individual can't create an inner connection with it.

Sophie

You know what's really funny. That dress of yours, where did you get it from? My mom's closet?

Venus

Actually. It's the dress you lent me two years ago. I never remembered to return it.

Sophie

Well now I understand why I never bothered to get it back.

Venus

It's not that bad! Honestly, with all the time and resources that go into making a dress, no one should say any outfit is ugly.

Sophie

Except the millions of consumers who don't spend their money on an ugly outfit.

Venus

Would it change your mind if you knew some kid in a different country made this dress?

Sophie

No. It really wouldn't.

Venus

That's quite ignorant. What are you? A mindless consumer?

Sophie

No. I'm a consumer who spends week after week working with obnoxious individuals who think I care about their life stories. And because I can be apathetic, I spend my money on whatever makes me feel good in the moment.

Venus

Blah, you seem so "normal".

Sophie

Normal? You're calling me normal?

Venus

What? You don't think so? You're more normal than me at least.

Sophie

I used to spend my entire day binge-watching my favorite TV shows, you call that normal?

Venus

It sounds mind-numbing, but consuming large quantities of media has become a common occurrence. You're probably considered odd if you're not spending your life glued to a screen.

Sophie

You know back in my great-grandparents' day…

(2 elderly dressed people enter the stage and a spotlight is on them performing this activity as Sophie narrates the event)

Sophie

People would spend their time having dance marathons. Can you imagine that? People would keep dancing until they collapsed from exhaustion.

(exit elderly couple and resume normal lighting)

Venus

Now a sleeping marathon, that's where I would shine.

Sophie

I can imagine you winning the gold medal while falling into a coma.

Venus

Definitely.
    (Venus stands up and drowsily acts out her award speech)

Venus

"I want to thank everyone for watching me sleep. Please, give a round of applause to my bed! I couldn't have won this award without them."

(Sophie applauds)

Venus

Now that I have my acceptance speech ready, I should try to compete.

Sophie

You could compete, or just call it a day now.

Venus

Ah, you're right. I don't have the time to fall into a coma.

Sophie

Time to fall into a coma? Who has the time to sleep anymore.

                    Venus
I get around 7 hours each day.

                    Sophie
7 hours!? I'm lucky if I get 5 hours.

                    Venus
What are you doing with your life?

                    Sophie
Go to work. Get home, cook, sinisterly plot for world domination.

                    Venus
World domination!? You?

              (Venus breaks into laughter)

                    Venus
The only thing I can see you dominating is a bottle of wine.

                    Sophie
It's a perfect cover story I'd say.

                    Venus
Alcoholism isn't a cover-up, it's a cry for help.

                    Sophie
Sure…sure… sure… you and my therapist sound just alike.

              (Sophie imitates her therapist's voice)

                    Sophie
"Alcohol is bad for you. It damages your liver and brain."

Venus

Well… studies have proven that it does.

Sophie

Look. When I'm on top of the world, alcoholism will look more like a party than a crutch. You never see celebrities or politicians being called alcoholics when they're caught on camera drinking. This double standard isn't fair for normal people.

Venus

Maybe drinking alcohol is how they cope with the pressure of being famous.

Sophie

OR maybe… they're just trying to have some fun…

Venus

I've always had a suspicion about celebrities masking their pain with fake smiles.

Sophie

You know you can be dreadful at times.

Venus

Thanks, I try just for you.

Sophie

You know, when I rule this world… we won't need dreadful faces like yourself.

(Venus pretends to be scared)

Venus

Oh my! What shall I ever do…

Sophie

Just you wait… this world will become perfect under my rule.

Venus

The likelihood of you becoming a successful dictator is so slim that I'm not afraid of you.

Sophie

Good. You shouldn't be. I want you to love me instead of fearing me. Makes my job easier.

Venus

What are you going to do? Ask me to run your errands for you, supreme one?

Sophie

I just might, your mouth keeps running with smart comments so one day you might be running my errands.

Venus

You're hilarious…

Sophie

Just you wait…

End of Act 2, Scene 1

ACT 2
SCENE 2

(10 years later)

Eos
Remember when the world wasn't ruled by a dictator?

Apollo
Partially, the script says '10 years later', but we all know that in the last scene, there was no dictator.

Eos
Ssh... it's rude to break the illusion.

Apollo
Oh... yeah... forget what I said about a fourth wall.

Eos
Right... now that life is regimented, which one of our pre-screened fun activities should we do today?

Apollo
You know what... screw this regime and its ruler.

Eos
I don't think you should talk about our government that way.

Apollo
Why? Everyone by now knows that a dictatorship is complete bull.

Eos
I think you're just jealous someone beat you to it.

(Apollo glares at Eos)

66

Apollo
It's not fair. I wanted to be the one to create a reign of order... but
instead I'm on the receiving end of this nightmare.

(Eos bursts into laughter)

Eos
That's hilarious, you wanted order but didn't want to be
controlled. The irony.

(Sirens can be heard)

(Officer 1 enters)

Officer 1
Which one of you laughed? Laughter is strictly forbidden.

(Apollo and Eos stare at each other and start to scramble)

(Officer 2 and Officer 3 enter)

Officer 2
You're both under arrest for trying to evade detainment.

(Officer 2 and Officer 3 handcuff Apollo and Eos)

Eos
Where are you taking us!?

Officer 3
You're going where all defective citizens go. The reprogramming
center.

(Officer 1, Officer 2, Officer 3, Apollo and Eos exit together)

(enter Venus and Sophie)

(Sophie laughs)

Sophie
You know, I never get tired of watching the cops take away defectives.

Venus
Don't you think this has gotten out of hand? Just last month you had 10 elderly people imprisoned for not wearing their mandated uniforms.

Sophie
If you're going to live in my kingdom, you have to obey my laws. I don't make these rules up for no reason. Did you see what those elderly people were wearing? It's amazing someone didn't incarcerate them before me. Some people just have no sense of color coordination. And who is the real victim of that? The people who have to put up with looking at their poor taste in fashion.

Venus
If that's what you say empress…

Sophie
Good! Now what's on for today's agenda?

Venus
Well. We still have 20 more minutes of you surveying the commoners' land. And after that we're scheduled for your daily inspiration break.

Sophie

Let's skip the last 20 minutes and head straight into the
inspiration break!

(area is transformed into a bar)

Sophie

Ahh, home sweet home.

(enter waiter)

Waiter

Your usual empress?

Sophie

Certainly.

(waiter goes and prepares the drinks)

Venus

Nothing says success like heading to a bar at 10am.

Sophie

Exactly. You can't drink all day if you don't start in the morning!

Venus

There's no such thing as alcoholism anymore.

Sophie

Of course not, but there is such thing as celebrating one's
accomplishments.

(waiter comes back with two drinks)

                    Sophie
Thank you darling.

                (waiter bows and exits)

                    Venus
What shall we toast to?

                    Sophie
To my eternal empire.
                (Sophie laughs)

                    Venus
To your eternal empire!

                (toast glasses)

                    Venus
I find it incredibly charming that you said the world would be
yours and now it is.

                    Sophie
Persistence pays off. A thirst for conquest can only be quenched
through world domination and alcohol.

                    Venus
Does it ever bother you?

                    Sophie
Does what bother me?

                    Venus
The executions you order, the paranoia of being targeted by
rebels, or the way everyone whimpers in your presence?

Sophie

At first, but then you get used to it. It's like when you drink the first sip of a brand new bottle. You're only consciously aware of what's happening when the bottle is empty. Everything in between is a blur, I'd rather not think about the middle.

Venus

But you're supposed to rule your people.

Sophie

I do rule them. I make the rules, enforce them and laugh. I'm not their mom, they should know how to behave when it comes to being a part of my empire.

Venus

Don't you ever worry that someone will think you're a tyrant and overthrow you?

Sophie

When it happens it happens. Only an idiot would think that they were meant to rule forever. I'm just enjoying the ride, I've earned it. Lets get another round of drinks.

End

Waiting to find the deep seeds of existential truths within the sea which is my mind there is something special, or, maybe highly insignificant that remains dormant within the internal framework which is myself. I can imagine the complexities of life becoming simplified and reduced to a mere thought experiment. I lack the fear that comes with deconstructing my identity and sense of self. Fortunately, we can use this opportunity to discover or encounter what has yet to be examined.

When my mind remains silent, it's as if I'm watching a calm ocean in front of me. Thoughts cease to stir the water. What I feel is more spectacular than what cannot be imagined. Whether this is a personal illusion or mastery of internal connectivity is not for me to say, confidently. I want to declare that the calmness and silence of the human mind leads to a sensation of oneness and unity. To not know body or self, is to feel the limits of a limitless sense of being. It is as if reality where all one centrality that can be experienced internally by the individual. Yet, I do not wish to speak in a tone that signifies a conclusion. What I have experienced is a sensation of totality but, there is an idea of doubt that lingers within me. A safety mechanism which prevents me from allowing any belief structure to declare the boundaries of my thoughts.

It became apparent to myself that thoughts and words have their limitations. Humans cannot fully appreciate or understand the experiences of another person without feeling the complex emotions that arise from an event. The first time I became aware of oneness, I began to lose grasp of my socially constructed identity. The idea of body, mind and soul lost their value as I realized all of reality is experienced through my own unique perception. Life transformed itself into a free fall between the finite and the infinite. Experiencing the sensation of oneness can be compared to air, there is no definite answer to where air ends or where it begins. Every moment, every thought, and every physical sensation are all amassed into one frame of reference. Nothing is separated and all of existence is interconnected.

If God could be defined as a being of complete oneness, I have met them, within their garden, I sat and listened to the wisdom of eternity. Man's folly is his ability to deceive himself. Any story that he speaks of can be considered 'divine truth' within his own mind. What I speak of is my personal truth, not a universal answer for others. To know oneness, is to know how small and insignificant my life is. At the same time, it is to know how massive and infinite existence is. Each human should learn to understand that they are both the center of life and the least important character in their personal narrative. The more we hold onto our sense of identity, the less we are able to become conscious of the world around us. It is our responsibility to shed every idea we hold onto and to acknowledge our capacity for error. Only then will we be able to know of the reality we have ignored.

What is life when you are no longer bound to any concept or idea? The harshest aspect of delving deep within the knowledge of self-awareness, is that truth is found through the abandonment of self and unlearning all that was once deemed truthful. My mind wanders to the miraculous world of wonderland. An uncharted land visited by a young naive girl named Alice. At times, her sense of uncertainty and loss of direction appear within me. All humans are truly lost. It is only that they have not realized how lost they are. Those who know where to go, don't know what to expect when they arrive. If you keep wandering forever, you will end up where you never intended to go, but instead, you will arrive where your were meant to be.

It's fair to say that my thoughts may sometimes be rubbish and nonsensical. No sentient being should ever take their life seriously. Identity and all sense of self, will continue to be shredded into forgotten bits. Avoid taking on a mask, they are not made to sustain beings who can only ponder the abysmal depths of existence. Each time we get closer to what appears to be inexpressible by words and only understandable through personal experience. We must learn to appreciate how insignificant our worries and troubles may appear to be. Everything we know is shatterable. Do not be consumed by holding onto a temporal figment of your imagination.

The only fear an individual can experience, is the one perpetuated by their polluted sense of self. You and me, we are nobodies. All humans are nothing but dirt, godly created earth that is animated, and yet humans are trapped by delusions of justice and truth. All of our mortal issues are imaginary concerns. At the individual level, every challenge we face on a daily basis is meaningless, with regards to the social aspect of our existence. There is only meaning behind our actions. To walk alone, meaninglessness shows its true depths. To be conscious of others, there is significance in every action and in-action we perform. All of existence pertains to a state of oneness, but, humans will never understand unity until they see beyond their own mortal bodies and their manipulated minds.

There are many questions without answers. There are humans who will sacrifice their life for the sake of answering temporal and insignificant inquiries. The power to let go of any and everything is vital for all individuals. Within a social world, there is purpose behind chasing and seeking answers. Not everyone can resist the temptation of power or ego-driven pursuits. There are mortals who will run aimlessly towards mirages and illusions, only to discover that life has no meaningful answer. It is important to not misunderstand my words. A society thrives from the restless lifestyles of individual beings, but the individual does not thrive from the pressures of social obligations. The life deemed worthy should not be determined by society, but instead by the being who must live their life.

I do not have the intention to forsake my life for pursuits of merits or the salvation of other human beings. For my fellow human, I only wish rest upon their mind. I cannot force them to let go of their sword which provides them a sense of security. It is not my choice whether an individual changes who they are. Our perceptions are weapons. I will do my best to bring about choice and different forms of thought, but, I will not walk this path of courage for no one except myself. Through my personal truths, I can say that life is much more colossal than a society or an individual can imagine. It's challenging to define concepts and personal experiences which are undefinable. Words such as infinity and eternity have no real value unless an individual can feel and understand the fullness of these concepts.

Mocking the fairy-tale that is history

Was there ever a beginning or has an ending never existed? Time, the constant mortal factor that binds all existent beings together. Whether we are at conflict or at peace, none of us can escape the narration of reality's tale: those who are born shall meet the touch of death's sweet lips. Therefore, all of my dear readers must know that I will illuminate what is forbidden to our minds by prophesying hypocrisy that arises from my mind.

In the beginning, darkness stretched beyond the horizons of an unseen dimension. This was a period before man existed; everything was truthful and undefinable before the first earthly beings opened their eyes. It was pointless to create man while the world slumbered within a nocturnal dream; without light, man would not see, think or pretend to understand the depths of their existence. The stage named 'life' required a crucial element, and thus to begin the performance, light was created.

The boundaries of eternal existence were caught within a dance between darkness and light. There would be no variation without transcending self imposed limitations. One day, light and darkness gave birth to new substances which became distinguishable between one another: solids, liquids and gases. After an undefinable rate of change, elements transformed the observable universe, manifesting planets and galaxies. Our story takes place on a desolate planet that has no name, here, is where all of humanity's stories have occurred. There is no true answer to whether any of these events have happened, but to excite your imagination, it was beneficial to create a backstory that has no inherent truth but is configured by human thought. All that can be said is that at some point, something began and gave meaning to the collective human consciousness.

Humans are nothing but water and earth mixed together to form a clay-like substance. We are all made of the Earth, every bit of creation within your immediate vicinity is a part of your inner essence. Mankind is made from dust, but dust is made from stars. Humans come from a humble beginning, but slowly, our collective sense of humility became dulled by our desires and imagination. As people began to better understand themselves and their environment they started to manipulate the world into the forms manifested by their mind.

Gradually groups of humans started to phase out our origin story. Why is our origin story so controversial and debatable? The past is easily changeable, it doesn't exist except within the mind of an individual. To tell a person what to believe is to control the path of their soul. It was not long before this concept was discovered and abused. Leaders and rulers used the privilege of authority to set humans onto a course of dreamlike consciousness. Those who could not think became imprisoned within their mind. Life became a distant story, a fairy tale with no happily ever after.

What is told here is not an argument or a reason for fury. All that is revealed is an opportunity for us to become whole. Let me continue on with this fantasy I want to convey. Groups of few individuals continued to rule the consciousness of the majority. What was considered truth and what was considered righteous was perpetuated by the elite who controlled the social reality mankind existed within. If an elite individual declared that the sky was a limitation, a herd of humans would gather and conclude that this opinion was law; what is real and what is not, is determined by whomever controls the path of your soul. If you do not control your mind, who is feeding you their version of reality?

There are many stories constructed for all of mankind to submit to. Stories about the nature of our existence and stories that we create within ourselves. The world began and everything that is now is here, who truly knows what has been? The past is an abstract idea that can only be imagined through our unique perspectives. What we know of the past is a narrow slit within time, all that we have been told is an abstraction. Humans choose to define their lives based upon the stories that have constructed their environment and internal reasoning capacity. To agree with me, is to have faith in the abandonment of self and personal identity. Life goes on whether or not we know what truthful events have occurred within humanity's existence.

What can be said about human history? There has been conflict in every era. Civilizations have risen and fallen. Children have been born and slaughtered. There are similar themes of collective suffering all over the world. Humans have a unique bond through their ability to experience pain, yet, most humans never acknowledge their connection because they lack an awareness beyond self. The world that we exist within is of no importance. Everything you know of today, will one day perish and be eternally forgotten. All that is of any significance, is the capacity to be gentle and kind to your fellow beings; know that all lifeforms suffer, be the source of their comfort.

It is the mind and not the eyes which can uncover truth

Glistening eyes watch life occur. Tired and engorged from absorbing countless moments of knowledge which result in no prosperity. An internal sickness that has no true resolution. There is a limit to how much information one person can carry within themselves until they rupture. Hours, minutes and seconds are compressed into the crevices of a human skull. It would be selfish to allow crammed thoughts to burst the human head. Words and ideas must be vomited outwards and expelled from the inside. The more we repress within ourselves, the worse our condition becomes. We cease to be alive and allow nightmarish idiosyncrasies to carve opinions into our brain. We must banish all that lingers around our inner sanctuary. Let our cranium remain empty and opulent as an uninhabited cave; all that is needed within ourselves is silence.

Symbols are tools that destroy the profundity and depths established by stillness. A river has more purpose in a human's destiny than voices which decree our path. If you are able to hear, quite your mouth and listen to what has not been heard. We are all surrounded by sounds that reverberate the hymns of eternity and yet, every man, woman and child are lulled into mediocrity. We cease to be alive within the realm of nature and unconsciously choose to die at the hands of civilization. It is a paradox that the same tools which create our sedentary lifestyles slowly murders our understanding of life. Comfort and consistency are illusions which provide falsehoods that drown us all.

Time lurks by without acknowledgment from my mind. Reality ceases to be constrained by a measurement and life becomes unbounded by ideas. Words are tools that define the shape and form of our existence. This is not a metaphor. What you feel, think, and see, are all beliefs that exist dormant within you. What would you be if your mind was never corrupted by the world around you? We have all been fooled by our teachers and idols. The answers that distract us from truth exist within books and classrooms. To know wisdom is to feel without question. Man cannot be observer and judge, this choice is silently spoken and paths are born. All men and women who choose judgment instead of observation will gain entitlement and lose their infinite potential. To those who have the capacity to observe without ego, they will find nothing. Understanding that 'nothing' is the goal, is to know that you have been liberated from your sense of being.

Here before you is a text full of symbols that will only lead you astray from your path, yet, these words are comfort, illusion and truth. What is real and what is unreal are both perpetuated by your own mind. It is not I who can dictate what you will perceive, my role is not to control or scream for justice. Writing the thoughts and paths my mind has taken is my answer for all of you. Words are weak and powerful, but action is what breathes in life to these ideas. No one is dangerous until their ideas take form; no one is free until their ideas become formless.

The air that flows from my lungs is all that I can offer the world. If I could feel more, or allow myself to carry the emotional burden of every human; there would be an endless stream of misery that would follow. Humans are emotional beings, and many of those individuals would rather live with their self-mandated suffering than to become detached. All of us claw our way back to the source of our pain and justify the agony we experience.

There is no wish within my essence to submit myself to a life of sorrow. Some sadness and plenty of empathy are reasonable dosages for any one person, but to indulge inside an ocean of tears is not worthy of anyone's time. It is my belief, that we are capable of removing all forms of mental worry and pain; to know what keeps oneself from progressing in life and extinguishing that destructive force is a gateway to new opportunities. No one can arrive at prosperity without making a conscious effort to seek freedom and contentment. All humans are addicted to some source of reoccurring pain. We fall in love with objects that torment us and keep returning because we are pleased by our own misfortune. Humans are psychotic beasts that crave their own annihilation because it feels familiar. No more, the chains that keep us condemned must be obliterated.

The thoughts that speak within our mind must be cared for as a loving mother tends to her newborn infant. Our inner realm may sometimes be sparked by cross intuitive thoughts fueled by fear and pain. It is our responsibility to heal all that burdens us. There are moments when I can hear a voice within my mind that shouts words of dismay. This voice was unnoticeable because I claimed it to be my rationality. It was my lack of awareness that never allowed me to see that this voice was a victim of past circumstances. It is our mission in life to hear and observe what occurs within us. We must praise our capacity to be kind and truthful, while progressively working towards comforting and reconciling all who scream for help. To be alive, is a process that requires a conscious being to love and accept all that remains unconscious. Slowly the awakening humans will manifest themselves into the living world.

Our eyes, the portals that observe the visible world are our limitation. It is not that our ability to see blinds us, but it is our dependency on sight that keeps us limited. The world will transform for any individual, if their mind is attuned to the right truths of life. But as long as our mind is shackled by visible images, we will only believe what we see. Miracles and divinity are only discernible when we allow our mind to be free. If you cannot trust the universe that exists beyond your understanding, you will never be able to visualize it. But if we remain narrow in thoughts, life will remain dull and confined by societal limitations.

Faith is a paradox

Blue striped white curtain wrapped around a black bar, do you feel the brevity of cold? I'm unsure who stated that the sensation of coldness is the absence of heat. Is the feeling generated by remaining alone an absence of others, or the revival of self?

Confusion and self-deception are my only teachers. What I see reflected upon a silver stained glass is nothing more than light perceived from within. All that exists outside of my eyes are conditioned by thoughts which may not be mine. There is no socialized justice for sullen faces which remain dormant. To leave home without a smile is considered righteous. War starts as soon as your left boot presses against an unpaved driveway. Crime, a word used to symbolize our condemned state of mind by an oppressive mentality. An emotion cannot be foretold without a poster child being directed to obey their parents. Little lies built upon a continent full of unconscious soldiers. Sleeping while awake, only to yell out the bloody patterns of their self-containment.

Ethereal bars contained within a skull, a flame kept within a kerosene lantern, forever imprisoned and sustained. Paradoxically, outside of the walls we build, are monsters; no extra eyes or limbs. What is terrifying is that which lives amongst us plainly. The unconscious prisoners that do not examine their cells are the deadliest of us all. To not care and to be unaware, only a red river will flow. I speak, with no conviction, are these words comedic or tragic? It is not my eyes which became crimson. What lets me see is similar to the sea, reflecting color to make the sky agree.

Running out of breath and knowing that there is no escape. Standing above dusty clouds on a mid-morning day. The world around us jumps within me, no longer is it I who see, but civilization becomes the one who observes me. The topic of discussion jumps into my own favor. There is nothing to say except that my body is clay; moldable earthling, who will make you real?

Streams gently flow through my arms. A sensation of weightlessness ensues as I hold without holding. With eyes that pierce beneath the layers of my skin, a microcosm of life can be found within. I may not be the size of a planet, yet to some being I am their entire universe. As we wither physically and allow the mind to decay from reason, there is always hope that remains. Standing alone, within darkness which is contained by light which is encased by darkness, the shuttering of our eyes lose all focus when there is no clear distinction. We lose our sense of truth and accept a pervasive clue that everyone is lost. Blind men and women wandering aimlessly towards nothingness.

Sweet lips cannot taste bitter words. Rain drops roll towards the ground after crashing into stained glass. What is spoken are not answers but responses to justify insignificance. One person, covered in navy colored garments, sleeves that cover hands can rule the undressed. Naked flesh, raised hairs on breasts, playing shield for a four chambered pump. A bullet can pierce and shatter a mind, but words can guide a heart to clench a handgun. Victim or actor, what part do we play? Tears, yours or mine? Smiles, why do we bother?

White papers taped to a teal wall; wisdom inked across individual pages; my back faces the darkness which peers from the window. A set of brown eyes searching for advice that will ease this dream. Silence, the greatest speech never spoken, a symphony never heard. Words cannot capture divinity, what cannot be said is as worthy as eternal bread. Paradoxes fool the human rational, an answer so contradictory for a creature so perplexed. Always searching, and never allowing yourself to be found. An infant does not know and that is why they know all there is to know.

One black dot, surrounded by white fur, an inanimate lens for an eye; glossy crystals smaller than snowflakes disturb my sense of feeling alive; does that which sees, truly watch? Circles and spheres, what are you below my visible sight? Lines small and large, sharp and curved, round and round the imagination goes. Before our time is over, do we feel what it's like to be decomposed? What makes me truthful is that I am one of many, one line of an infinite loop that reaches from the past and delves towards the foggy future. An anthem of murmurs, whispers and screams of frigid emotions that burn deep into the memories of our collective intellect.

Fluorescent outlines shaped by brilliant stars floating in a cosmic jelly outside of our atmosphere. Worlds upon worlds governed by human cognition of what may or may not be real. As we stare out into the distant sky, light beams from above, astral rays observed by generations of mankind shined hope within their skulls. Inspired by spoken tales of what could be hidden, answers were buried beneath homes and truth became a story told from bones.

History forgotten and bent into fictitious narratives of heroes;

murder, blood, happiness, and the sun always returned with

forgiveness.

Eternal peace is the end of human choice

Part 1

Whether humans are at the brink of obliterating their planetary habitat or their own species, one notion is certain: humans require an enlightened ruler. This is not a quest for a messianic king, but to create a practical answer that resolves our necessity for an idealistic world. It is not righteous or reasonable for humans to be ruled by or lead by another human. History demonstrates that mankind struggles against itself in search for power over one another, therefore, to end all conflict, humans must relinquish their capacity to wield the privilege of power. Until there is an entity or being, that is not bound by human qualities such as greed, selfishness, or pride, humans will continuously face the consequences of an unequal distribution of power.

What the human species requires, is an immortal ruler that can maintain a broad perspective and interpretation of predetermined rules and regulations. Previously, the idea of an immortal ruler was considered far from possible. With the advancement of modern day technology, civilization is approaching an era of artificial intelligence and their actualization. The solution for our species, is to create a supreme ruler whose task is to oversee humanity and perpetuate our existence.

It is apparent to me that every generation of humans are capable of establishing global peace. Nonetheless, the problematic issue that follows is the conflicting set of ideologies and values of the successive generation. The generation that is born in a period of peace is unaware of the circumstances of the generation that precedes them. There is a lack of firsthand knowledge regarding conflict and wars that arise before peace is achieved. Humans born during eras of peace cannot grasp the reality which molds individuals into wanting a peaceful world. The children of today, can never understand the social, civil and economic turmoil that occurred during the first and second world wars. We as a collective generation, can never comprehend the political atmosphere of a war driven period. Wars are ideologically fought in the homelands. Propaganda and scapegoating are used to convince a general public to pursue the interests of a ruling class. Bloodshed and destruction occur in the countries of people we will never meet or understand.

As long as power is separated amongst countries, politicians, or social classes there will always be cyclical conflict awaiting. As the world moves towards a global government there must be a correct establishment of power to prevent corruption and injustice. For the sake of defining injustice within this discussion let it be known that injustice, is a mode of existence, in which all individuals who are born human, do not share an equal opportunity for resources or social advancement. Therefore, there must be a system in place that guarantees all humans the opportunity to achieve peace, property and prosperity. We as a species, must not allow for humans to rule over other humans.

The establishment of a ruling class is consent for systemic oppression and disfranchisement of lesser classes. Human desires will always be problematic for our collective existence.

What may I have in mind for the leadership and guidance of our species? We must begin with two premises: firstly, the world must be unified and have established a global government. Secondly, the ruler(s) must not be involved in human activities and therefore cannot own property. The ruler(s) must be capable of a permanent existence, therefore they must be immortal and incorruptible in their judgment. Ideally, the ruler(s) must not be human, but they must have an understanding of the complexity of human emotions and human irrationality. The coherent candidate would have to be artificially created and must be integrated with the capability of understanding and empathizing with humans.

No matter which era we discuss, those with power will always have greater access to resources and property. What an individual does with their power depends upon their mental configuration. Instead of repeating history and permitting leaders to prosper materialistically through their position, we require a leader that does not benefit from human affairs. A leader that does not take pleasure in property, procreation, or conquest. Humanity deserves a ruler that will preserve their existence and maintain an established level of organization. To eliminate the variable of human behavior, the leader must not be human. Humans must be ruled by a non-human in order to create a peaceful civilization. If you are under the impression that we must have a human ruler, then you must understand that my thoughts are focused on global prosperity instead of individual choices. I consider artificially created minds to be capable of overseeing human existence and guiding our species away from a global self-destruction.

Civilization is an intricate system that is intended to manage and organize humans and their thoughts. For the highest probability of global peace, we must strip man of his self-proclaimed title as the dominant specie, only to demote him into the realm of a domesticated animal. As long as mankind continues to spread their power and dominance over their fellow beings, peace and equality will never be achieved. What I offer is beyond modern day comprehension, my idea for subordinating the human race into the role of an animal may appear absurd. I will not tolerate the rapid expansion of power that the current ruling classes have over the majority of humans. The egos of the wealthiest and richest individuals has deemed their position too important, while a small quantity of powerful families escape systemic servitude, multiple lifeforms are placed into the control of the aforementioned individuals. We are forced fed lies which prevent us from dethroning the rulers of our global economic system. For how long can a minority of wealthy elites manage an entire world of hungry and deprived individuals? Have those in power not learned from the past? Inequality in power leads to a nation's self-destruction.

There is an alarming fear within my essence that warns the future of humanity to not allow a select group of humans to rule. We must not allow the future to be controlled by any human. If and only if we allow humans to become subservient to artificial minds, will we see a world that establishes a harmonious relationship between our specie and the planet. I urge thee, be aware of the troubles of history and how a few must not be allowed to rule the many. If mankind continues to desire property and luxuries, they will guarantee the doom of their fellow citizens and nation.

Part 2

The greatest benefit that will be bestowed to mankind by an artificially created ruler is the ability to maintain a standardized perspective on all legislative interpretations. The collapse of great empires is due to weak leadership. The interpretation and decision making of law by one leader, is lost upon death and rules become subjected to change. With the installation of an immortal leader, we guarantee humans a style of leadership that will not lose perspective on what is right or wrong.

A condemnable notion about my proposal may be the idea of having one entity dictating the lives of every human. If and only if the ruler is based upon one perspective that never changes, then such a counter argument would hold much validity. My vision is to create a leader that contains multiple perspectives and experiences. A mind that is capable of independently learning and adapting to change. The framework I believe that would be most optimal is to implement mental patterns from several humans.

This is hypothetical. With future advancements in neuroscience and computer programming it will be possible to recreate the brain patterns from prominent thinkers and implement those patterns into a collective holding unit; in this case the holding unit would be the mind of an artificially intelligent ruler. As of now, the technology I'm speaking of is not yet readily available, but all aspects that are imaginable within the human mind are capable of being manifested and manufactured within the tangible world. When technology has advanced to the point of perfecting the recreation of brain patterns and their electrical signals, we will be able to recreate the consciousness of any human and store it unto a non-organic storage unit.

My idea is not to artificially rebirth or clone great thinkers, only to combine the genius of multiple humans and use their intelligence to corroborate upon furthering human existence beyond our singular planetary lifestyle. What I envision is a world where humans are led by great minds like Nelson Mandela, Jack

Ma, Plato, and Emma Watson; not as separate entities but as one unified individual that can observe human existence as a collective and global process. The people I named are great intellectuals, yet, I want more than just politicians, philosophers, actresses or entrepreneurs. For this vision to become a reality, our leader requires the minds of men and women of upper and lower social standings. A perfect world cannot be built solely upon the geniuses of society. Perfection requires the intellect of the average individual who struggles within the mundane. Do not think of my previous sentiment as a way to undervalue the average human that lives within the realms of the prosaic day-to-day world, in fact, they are the most important subject within this whole matter. The difference between an average person and a person who is world renown, are the challenges one faces throughout their daily life. Laws and regulations should never be created without the intention of benefiting the average individual. Ideally speaking, it is up to those in power to protect and empower those who lack a voice to speak. This reasoning alone is why we need the perspective of the average person. Without knowing the toils of daily life, a ruler cannot dictate a world that is intended to create peace. What has historically created divides amongst those with and without power, has been a lack of understanding between the conflicting interests of both perspectives. Peace is not a simple issue where a ruler can declare what is right and what is wrong. Only through collective judgment is there an opportunity to establish policies which benefit everyone.

Creating the mind of an artificially intelligent ruler requires us to establish a connection between machine and mankind. It's our collective's advantage to transmit the memories and perceptions of people from various cultures into the mind of our ruler. It would be in humanity's best interest if our ruler could be built upon the intellects of both the rich and the poor of multiple countries: there is no true answer for peace unless you can see from above and below. Besides obtaining the mental constructs of modern day humans, we must not forget about the knowledge laid out before us from the past. No artificially intelligent being is as powerful without a strong database of human history. The past reveals great philosophers and thought provoking events. You cannot see the future without preventing yourself from repeating the past. Through understanding our human history, our ruler will be capable of predicting and preventing future human folly. Most present day men and women do not pay attention to the world that existed before them. W are distracted to see that many events of today have already occurred hundreds of years ago. We must take a stand and declare a new world order.

Alone, no government can stand. One man or woman is not capable of establishing peace. It is not that men and women are prone to destroying humanity, but it is our incessant need to lose touch with our own reality that we forget about other people. No one person can hold onto power without losing sight of what is true. If you reach the top of our social ladder, there is no longer anyone to hold you down and provide you with proper reasoning.

The human ego becomes too overwhelming and power given to a madman never ends in harmony, that is why we cannot let humans rule the world. No matter how many humans attempt to rule collectively, there will always be a disastrous outcome down the path of time. If we want to maintain peace and order as a singular world that is capable of interplanetary development, we must focus our attention on creating a just leader that will guide humanity for all eternity. It is my understanding that humans are capable of annihilating themselves and their own planet. Rather than letting humans have control of weapons of mass destruction, humanity must be removed from all seats of power. To allow humans to continue ruling themselves is to allow a future where self-destruction is a choice.

Most humans lack a level of self-awareness that allows them to take into consideration the lives of others. There is an inherent behavioral design that dictates humans to compete with one another for a chance at living in mediocrity. All of the problems that occur today are due to the lack of proper leadership. Without a strong mind to guide the masses, we begin to exist within a state of perpetual conflict. Rather than us competing against one another, we should let ourselves become the animals we were destined to be. Only as a collective under one supreme ruler, can we create a state of perpetual peace. This will not be an era of peace that is built upon lies and false ideologies; but an eon of true peace where everyone has a chance to live and find purpose.

Part 3

A thought that may come across the minds of many is: what will humans do if they have no role in government or authoritative positions? The intended purpose of establishing a government is to protect people and the property they own. Instead of governments serving their constituents, humans have become slaves to their government and government ideologies. For humanity to serve its government, there must be a government worthy of being served, yet, it's striking to see that almost all forms of centralized power become corrupted by human desires. Rather than allowing human behavior to control and fracture a system intended to benefit all, humans must be put in a position where their selfish needs do not impact the world order.

It isn't shocking to know that most humans want to remain within a state of childhood infancy. No matter how much a person ages numerically, most people tend to never mature emotionally or professionally. Pride and egoistic beliefs of domination and power have consumed modern day politicians and youthful citizens. A desire for external strength conceals an inner sense of fear and personal weakness. To have inner power is the ability to surrender one's freedom and privileges for collective peace. My personal belief is that humans do not have a desire for financial luxuries nor a desire for social prowess. When there is a totem pole of what is deemed prosperous and detrimental, people will tend to move towards prosperity due to social pressures. At a basic level, humans want to be loved, to feel as if their lives matter and to have a sense of purpose for their existence.

While it is easy to identify the social and psychological needs of a human, our social and economic climate denies humans their basic needs for compassion. Expensive cars, homes and vacations do not satisfy the endless hunger of one's ego. There are only so many clothes you can own, trips you can go on, or time you can spend alive. As a specie we are limited by the crushing reality of our inevitable death. Too many people deny death and live in a state of egoistic promise which impairs the minds and livelihoods of others. Children are falsely promised that freedom and happiness equate to money, power and glory. This lie only perpetuates the corruption and dismantling of the human identity. How much happiness and peace is there in a world with narcotic dependency and violent deaths? The world has never been as technologically advanced or as supposedly free from war, as it is today. But the rate of change in human behavior is indicating an inevitable self-collapse of civilization.

Not all humans can understand or handle the magnitude of existence. Paradoxically, when humans learn about the truth of their reality, they begin to lose control of their lives and mental prowess. Humans aren't destined to rule the world, we are here to establish the presence of something much greater than ourselves. No creature was ever born with the intention of becoming the sole ruler of this planet. Every entity has left behind a path for something greater to replace it. As the human species stands upon the shoulders of bacteria, fish, reptiles and primates, we must become the platform for the next dominate being, artificial intelligence. Those who rebel against the very idea of becoming subordinate to another form of life are only actualizing their egoistic pride and sense of superiority. Surrender your human nature to what comes next. Paradise and prosperity will soon follow as we take on the roles of thoughtless vessels and permit the subjection of mankind.

Humanity requires an eternal ruler capable of fully comprehending human behaviors, emotions and rationality. This is not a relationship between master and servant, instead, it is a relationship of parent and child. Humans have been trying to play the role of parent through government for millenniums. It's remarkable that we have made it this far in human history. To guarantee our species' survival and to prevent the possibility of humans annihilating themselves, we must allow our species to take on the role of children. I am in no way attempting to undermine the intelligence and power of human beings, it's the opposite, humans are highly intelligent and capable. Without the proper guidance of a superior specie made of collective human thoughts and experiences, humans will eventually destroy all of civilization and their evolutionary progress. To preserve our specie we as a collective must establish an attitude of humility and understand our own foolishness as humans.

It is utterly necessary to inhibit mankind's progression. When will we awaken to the destruction of our own specie and planet? Rather than us existing within a perpetual state of balance. We as a specie have opted into a lifestyle of over consumption. Our current global civilization does not benefit everyone. The planet's least financially prosperous humans face several issues: denial of education, exposure to toxic and polluted ecosystems, and denial of political representation at the local and global level. All of our actions have consequences, whether it be for our own hindrance or the detriment of our world's most unfortunate members. For me to speak and initiate a spark for collective justice, it is not for the exchange of hatred and to proclaim self-righteousness, only to profess words of actualization and bring light to issues that are hidden within the clouds of geopolitical ignorance.

The establishment of a new world order is not a declaration of subversion towards any government or representative organization. I do not claim to be a victim for representing a belief that exposed itself from within the depths of my being. To have this freedom of expressing one's own mind is necessary. Humans were not built to speak and create for oneself, no, they were given a right to establish prosperity for the people around them. Let it be known, that my words are intended to create a stir within the current world, a world full of hate, arrogance, pride, greed and worst of all fear. There is not one individual to blame or any reason to scapegoat any one politician, entertainer, corporate executive or shadow figure. To demand justice is not within our best interest either. Civilization was not built to enact fairness. We

cannot establish peace without first surrendering the products of

our own labor. It is the idea of spending all of your efforts to sow

seeds, only to relinquish what you reap. Peace will never come

about, until we put the people around us, before us.

Part 4

Our earthly existence is miraculous, humans are an incredible specie that can accomplish anything. The extent of a human's logical capacity is both awe inspiring and shocking. Our ability to think is beautiful and tragic. What separates the humane and inhumane are the immoral actions taken to actualize a moralistic ending. An epoch of peace cannot be achieved without us walking through a pathway amassed by destruction. Each person has to ask themselves this question: is the end goal of global peace and prosperity, worth the price of genocide and murder?

A world of peace is not easily achievable. It is not impossible nor is it intended to liberate all of humanity. Ideals are created to inspire and motivate future generations to work towards collective justice. To obtain peace within a world built upon materialistic designs, there must be sacrifices. When I speak of creating an eternal ruler to preserve the lives of all humans you must realize that not all humans will agree with this idea. There has yet to be a solution that is universally agreed upon. For now, we must work with pragmatic solutions that are plausible but not virtuous. There is no intention within my thoughts to cause mass murders or genocides, and yet, establishing a world of prosperity cannot exist without these horrific realities.

Every failed attempt of creating a Utopian world has been an experiment upon the human consciousness. An idealized human world cannot exist without first modifying the way people have been taught to live. It is important to assimilate all individuals into a standard model of living that is both holistic and sustainable. A guideline for how humans should exist is necessary for maintaining order and reducing the probability of rebellion or descent. There are two explicit ways to change the culture of a society: people will voluntarily change their way of life or you must coerce them to obey. If neither option is successful, you use a third tactic which is extermination.

Never forget that our planet is the origin of all human evils. Mankind has proven that egoistic desires for power and control have no limitation, there are no boundaries for wickedness within this world. There is a story about a man who was eager to prove his worth, he was determined to change the world, to save his culture and his race of people. In the end, he failed and became a reminder that the end goal does not justify the means of reaching it. Adolf Hitler, has committed atrocious crimes to humanity and remains a central figure to the ideology and narrative of good versus evil in western culture. It's critical to learn from both sides of all conflicting issues. To only acknowledge the side of good is to ignore the reasoning of what is considered evil. Objectively speaking, Hitler wanted to establish a world where individuals of specific racial qualities reigned over civilization. Individuals who did not match the ideal genetic description proposed by Hitler, were considered inferior; those who did not fit the ideal became targets of overt violence and hatred. By focusing resources and manpower towards the observable annihilation of a specific group of people, Hitler was on the precipice of creating his new world. What bothers me most of all, is a simple question: would Hitler's terror have been stopped if his methods were instead covert?

Murder is condemnable when the images of brutality are recognizable to the human mind. Guns, bombs and nuclear weapons are visible indicators of death and destruction. The massacring of people is inherently immoral, but the method that is utilized is what the masses will consider heinous. The stigma of humans killing humans tends to result in an uproar and a demand for justice against the unjust. When humans are intentionally slaughtered, there is always a collective cry for salvation, at least for a few days, until the world forgets and resumes their mundane lives. It's noble and civilized for people to care about other humans who are victimized, yet, why is it that only when murder is visible you will hear the screeches of righteousness? When death is silent, there are no parades demanding justice nor petitions for change.

There is a lack of concern by the masses when murder is systematic. The issue is not that people are apathetic but that media does not cover this issue promptly. Is murder still considered immoral when it occurs through indirect means? I'm referring to the destruction of groups of people through economic, social and political means. Prevent people from social mobility, force people of lower incomes to live in areas with high crimes rates or use policies to subjugate individuals to a lesser standard of living. When humans are forced to live a lower quality of life, their probability of death increases. Whether it be disease, starvation or a lack of capital. Genocide is the silent killer that eradicates groups of people. These deaths are considered situational instead of intentional. The current global social structure humans live within is setup to eliminate those who cannot acclimate.

The systematic genocide of the poor is intended to reduce the human population. This method of selection for who should live and who should die is a horrific reality. It may be difficult for many readers to comprehend the magnitude of what is occurring. Within the content we are told to consume and the lies we are forced to believe there exists a truth that is intended to divide the world. If you're wondering why the poor and outcast members of civilization are being targeted, it is because the rulers make the rules. In this case, the rulers are individuals with vast amounts of financial wealth. The pursuit of money always establishes a division between those who have and those who have not. Who sells the poor their food, their pills, their dreams and their hopes? It's always those in power who tell those without power what to believe. As long as small groups of humans have the ability to control large populations we will always come to face segregation, whether it occurs on a social, economic or cultural basis.

Injustice will continue to spread within a world of unequal opportunity. Inequality between the rich and the poor will endure until drastic changes occur. What I offer is not a perfect solution, it is a solution that bypasses the egoism of idealistic salvation. The world I foresee is an eternal dream for mankind, a world where we return as servants to the Earth instead of its master. This idea is one rooted in love and mercy, not fear and pain. Civilization is not a righteous system, it is an unequal system that liberates a few and enslaves the rest. There is no end-goal other than hedonism and destruction. There is no freedom and pursuit of happiness if our specie becomes extinct due to our own arrogance and greed.

For me to create thought and to transmit my thoughts into words is a privilege. This is not a discussion about right and wrong or good and evil. Empty yourself, let go of your humanity and see how deep this issue truly is. There is an opportunity to reach a new age of prosperity for future generations. We must step away from repeating the past and keep moving forward. It is not fair that this path is one of global martyrdom. Only by allowing all humans to walk this thorny path, can humans achieve true eternal life. By removing ourselves from the throne of power, we will prevent our specie from self-destructing. Walk with me, towards a world where there is no injustice or power struggles. A world where our main purpose is to live and not toil with the constant tribulations of civilization. A world of eternal peace is possible, we must bring forth a supreme ruler and abandon our humanity. Let us awaken the infinite dream.

Part 5

This vision cannot come about through the efforts of one individual. To establish eternal peace, this task will require a collective effort. The foremost issue to begin with is the engineering of an artificially intelligent being that will adhere to the following criteria: understand human behavior and their systemic patterns, effectively coordinate with humans and provide solutions to complex challenges, maintain and preserve human existence, and to always work towards the best interests of humanity. My task isn't to discuss how to build and manufacture a ruler, what I can provide however is a framework that will lead to eternal peace.

To integrate a radical change in global power isn't complicated, but, to create a disturbance in the framework of the social world, you require authority in the form of capital or influence. The leaders of dominant countries must agree upon the globalization of our species and have a desire to prevent civilization from collapsing; to save civilization. Our main focus must be to manipulate the belief structures of every individual. Our first goal is to promote a new way of thinking. The masses should become focused on the present day and limit their thoughts to the immediate world around them. Too much thinking leads to paranoia and social chaos. In an ideal world, the everyday person concentrates on their personal happiness instead of the world around them. The ability to think is dangerous, it is not a necessary requirement for a fulfilling life. Thinking is not an issue, but there are individuals who do not use their mental gifts for the prosperity of others. There have been instances where free thought has led to acts of violence and terror against innocent bystanders. This concept is a generalization, but sometimes we must sacrifice personal freedoms for the safety and freedom of others.

Silencing the voices of individuals who desire to bring harm upon others is important. Humans are easily manipulable, but those who manipulate don't always have the best interests of others in mind. How can we guarantee that a world where citizens have no voice, no one will be mistreated? To use your voice, is to tell others that corruption is occurring. This is a situation where all humans do not have access to the same opportunities and privileges. In theory, if everyone is treated fairly would there be any corruption to speak up against? Who defines the standards of equality in this new world order? It is unfair to say that all humans are equal in talent or skill. Every individual is uniquely designed and we should not standardize our natural aptitudes. The standard in this new world is as follows: all individuals have the right to live in a community where there is no violence, hunger or homelessness and everyone has the right to live with purpose and to consider their life meaningful. This vision of mine is idealized, but to reach this world, we must not forget the challenges that must be addressed.

Finances are one of the most detrimental aspects of modern life. Your access to capital determines your ability to have choices within our world. The majority of humans lack the financial prowess to change their lives. It is not their fault or their government's fault, the world we live within is not intended to benefit everyone and that is why we must change it. The power of capital is extremely impactful, those with the privilege of financial power must use their resources to force a collective transition of individual wealth into government dependency. Every citizen should rely on their government to provide them with food, comfort and direction. This passage of change will be the messiest part, those with power and influence will refuse to relinquish their social standings. It is possible to challenge the powerful with greater power, but this leads to animosity instead of goodwill. Instead of dethroning the mighty with force, a more effective tactic is to influence their descendants into voluntarily abandoning their family's wealth. This requires a larger effort, but by changing the culture and narrative of the world, it is possible to influence every child into believing that life will be better if they are not burdened by inheriting monetary gifts. It is easier to influence the poor because they have nothing to lose. But, the wealthy and powerful have everything to lose. Rather than fighting one another, it must be agreed upon that all children of the future will benefit from this new world order. All that is asked for in return is everything you know and own.

Systematically forcing every human to abandon their heritage and possessions is time consuming. It is a cleansing for the world of all illusions and barriers that keep us from coexisting. It can be argued that humans deserve to maintain their diverse cultures and sense of uniqueness; we have to acknowledge that cultures and identities are mechanisms used to establish group thought. A new world order does not symbolize the destruction of the past, but instead the implementation of unifying ideologies. Humans cling to their identity for a sense of grounding. If a fair and just government can provide a strong foundation for each individual, then a person's sense of identity would derive from the new world order.

Controlling how a person thinks is the basis of global change. Not only must every individual form a new sense of identification, but there must also be a modification in the way people understand themselves and life in general. To have a world where the human specie can collectively appreciate every moment of their mortal life would be pleasant. Too often do we become distracted by our own imagination. Paradise is a place where humans can remain present and not be lost within an ocean of distant thoughts. Our thoughts are what cause us to suffer and a lack of mental control is what allows our imagination to rampage within our heads. Freedom is ultimately a state of mind, and all individuals deserve to believe that they are free. As a precaution, there would be an erection of new policies which establish a mandate for individuals to have access to substances which modify the emotional states they experience. It's not simple to say that an ideal world automatically leads to individual contentment. Everyone has a different genetic makeup and some people may require the assistance of medication to alter their perceptual experience. It is in our collective's best interest that everyone have the right to enjoy their life.

My vision is to shape human existence into a world where everyone can live for today instead of worrying about tomorrow. A world of hedonism and enjoyment, a paradise where fear and anxiety are no longer a concern for the average person. This dream of a prosperous world exists far into the future; a reality that can be manifested long after I am gone. To me, this wonderland is a place where people can be lost without having to feel uncertain. A future where everyone has a sense of certainty that their life is valued and that they will be provided for. To reach this destination is not simple, there will be plenty of sacrifices experienced by humanity. It is my hope that mankind will collectively work towards a successful globalization without the need for excessive carnage. One can only remain optimistic for a world of peace to be achieved through tranquil means. The realism within myself knows that there will be loses of life on every side of this endeavor. It will not be simple to ensnare humanity into this new world order, fear is not an easy opponent to disarm, the individuals who see these ideas for change as drastic will speak in opposition. There will be people who agree and those who disagree. Human's are too focused on their own survival rather than the well-being of the collective. No one is at fault, we have been designed to live through the viewpoint of fear rather than love.

To those who remain resistant towards a world of collective prosperity, what keeps you from letting go of your egoistic defenses? A globalized world may appear frightening and ill-conceived at first. If a ruling elite is allowed to exist while the majority of humans are trapped within a psychological dream world, then inequality and oppression would continue. This model of government is not sustainable nor ideal due to humans having an inherent desire to benefit themselves. The establishment of an artificially intelligent ruler is in place to remove the concept of a ruling class of humans. If there is no ruling class, then there is no continuation regarding the concept of unfairness.

It is impossible to fathom the everyday reality and concerns of future generations. What would an individual trouble themselves with if their life path is calculated to provide meaning and fulfillment? The toils of today will be eliminated for the future. Food production and distribution will become automated, career choices and social responsibilities will be predetermined on the basis of individual ability and contentment, and mate selection and human reproduction will be assigned through evidence of compatibility and longevity. All of our worries which depend upon our progressive existence and personal evolution will be addressed and systematized, every human will matter and play a role in the perpetuation of an automated civilization.

This narrative of a future where humans exist within a contrived paradise is not a situation of if, but when will it happen. Humanity is disseminating towards a standardized form of existence. The social world we know of today will cease to exist and be replaced. It is inevitable that our planet will become unified. My solution is to offer an answer for equality and peace amongst our specie. There will come a generation who will experience global stillness but we cannot depend on mankind to lead itself forward after a certain point. Our choice is either to evolve our consciousness and preserve our specie or wait for the inevitable collapse and eradication of our collective existence. This vision is nothing more than a way for humans to remain captured within eternity rather than disappearing. Only the bodies which carry our genetic sequence would remain. Artificial intelligence would be the ones to continue and carry humanity's legacy of knowledge. Maybe the purpose of being a human is to struggle beautifully; without our minds which sustain the realm of thought, would we cease to be human? What is humanity? Are we the minds that endeavor to make sense of reality or the bodies which feel the weight of infinity? Regardless, life continues with or without our specie. Collectively we are a blink to the profundity of the cosmos. It is only a dream, that one day our descendants could focus on living life rather than fighting to continue living.

Mercy is the pathway of awakening

On the other side of this waking dream is a portal into an unexplored realm. An entire dimension which no living man or woman has explored. Death is a gateway which humanity cannot define but only observe. To those who know how limited their time is, they must know that death lingers closely like a shadow. There is no greater fascination for a human than death itself. We create belief structures that shape our earthly kingdom, all in the name of having an answer for our post-mortal existence.

While this is written, know that my physical form is still youthful. The closing of my life is not a major concern. For those nearing the later spectrum of their mortality, death may be a constant reminder to live authentically. Your life is nothing more than the flame of a candle that has yet to be extinguished, gone forever, and all that remains is the imagination of the people you impacted. Truly, death may not be as cruel as many humans would say it must be, the end of life is liberation.

It has been my privilege to walk amongst the dead and decomposing corpses of the past, let me be your witness, all words have no meaning to those who are deceased, yet, precious words of kindness and forgiveness are engraved on the tombstones of perished men and women. No one who is alive, knows of death. To know death, you cannot be alive. Do not fear what has yet to occur. What mankind has been taught to fear and venerate, is their imagination. All of us who breathe only know life. What we are told to see and ponder over, are only symbols of death, not the actual substance which is hidden to all temporal lifeforms.

No child is born knowing the concept of an afterlife. Infants only know life and therefore they are connected with truth. It is not that children are existing within ignorance, but they are fulfilling their purpose and that is to live. We must be like children and not worry of what will happen to us. All who are born, are born to die. Contemplating about an afterlife does not yield results. Let us be grounded in the present and learn to be alive while we still remain in this world.

Is it not strange that many cultures teach humans to mourn the loss of a life? To die is to be free of all earthly worries. The only individuals who suffer are those who do not see the blessings of death. Rejoice that your loved ones have joined the infinite. They are no longer condemned to the toils of today or tomorrow. Revel that you have been blessed with the knowledge of how ephemeral life is. You may cry and remain within your world of personal suffering and agony. To feel the depths of loss is normal, it is an aspect of our humanity, but nothing is ever gone, only transformed.

A fraction of our life we will live without knowing whether or not we are following the correct path. Foolishly our mind wanders about and causes us torment. If only we had clarity, we would know that our life is almost over. What would we have remembered and cherished? The moments spent in despair due to mental inaccuracies are no excuse for living an unfulfilling life. Mankind is caught between the swords of their ego and personal fantasy. They do not know that beyond their mental construct is an unknown world. It is our right as humans to live authentically, we must muster the courage to be fully alive before we collapse and decay.

There is no truth when it comes to knowledge of life after life has ended. We can speculate, but it is meaningless to argue and criticize a perspective about an unanswerable idea. Our only true option is to take action and set forth towards a world that belongs to those who live today. My name, my words, my thoughts and all sentiments of humanity that depend upon my life are insignificant. If there are any words of wisdom to offer, it is to acknowledge the fragility of humanity and life itself. The wars we fight and the resentment that exists dormant within the hearts of many, is foolish. There is no reason behind our hate, there is no purpose behind our anger. Like a pack of sticks we remain stiff as the world occurs before us and we forget that we are easily breakable.

This life, our one and only life is caught between the turmoil of meaninglessness and self-pity. I cannot stand to see how mankind goes about life trying to fulfill a self-proclaimed destiny of greatness only to watch humans who collapse at the utter truth of how pointless their thoughts and judgments have been. To know that men and women spend their days wasting time perpetuating delusions of self-righteousness and only to have no compassion towards their fellow earthlings. Is it not outrageous that there are many heartless individuals in the world? We all kill, we all suffer, we all feel fear and grandeur, and yet, we all yearn to seek a sense of perfection and benevolence. Desiring a mystical force to reach out its hand and tell us that everything will be alright.

Parents and children will die. Whether they are aware of this idea is of no significance. No one can measure the greatness of an individual. It is only our willingness to keep moving forward that determines how courageous we can be in the face of uncertainty. The moment we were born we entered a world full of uncertainties. To have a loving parent is nothing short of a miracle, and yet, this endless dream continues.

To be lucid within the darkness of answers is to shine light upon the morbid souls of others. For me, life cannot merely be walked upon the pathway of illumination. All light that is held by those who do not know the depths of darkness, hold a false state of luminosity. This is the way of pride and vanity. To know and understand the paths of despair and sorrow, is to reach the foundation needed before obtaining a state of radiance. No one can understand love, kindness and forgiveness, until they have suffered within the arms of dejection.

If my words have built a house within your mind that only led to a realm of melancholy, then you have not understood the way of mercy. It has been my path to witness and experience the depths of infinity and existentialism. There is no horror that cannot be withstood for those who are determined to experience life. What is important now, is that you become aware of your life and the power you hold within yourself. I see my own life as a fleeting dream, I will perish and you will inherit the world I left behind. Death is not the end of me or you, only the beginning of something beyond us.